Weight Lifting
Log Book

Belongs to

_____

_____

_____

Date: _____   **Muscle Group:** _____

S M T W T F S   **Start Time** _____
◯ ◯ ◯ ◯ ◯ ◯ ◯

Weight: _____   **Finish Time** _____

☐ **Upper Body**   ☐ **Lower Body**   ☐ **Abs**

Exercise	Set	1	2	3	4	5	6	7
	Reps							
	Weight							
	Reps							
	Weight							
	Reps							
	Weight							
	Reps							
	Weight							
	Reps							
	Weight							
	Reps							
	Weight							
	Reps							
	Weight							
	Reps							
	Weight							

Cardio	Time	Distance	Heart Rate	Cals Burned

Measurements

Neck	R Bicep	L Bicep	Chest	Waist	Hips	R Thigh	L Thigh	Calf

Date:_____ **Muscle Group:** _____

S M T W T F S   **Start Time**_____
◯ ◯ ◯ ◯ ◯ ◯ ◯

Weight:_____   **Finish Time**_____

☐ **Upper Body**   ☐ **Lower Body**   ☐ **Abs**

Exercise	Set	1	2	3	4	5	6	7
	Reps							
	Weight							
	Reps							
	Weight							
	Reps							
	Weight							
	Reps							
	Weight							
	Reps							
	Weight							
	Reps							
	Weight							
	Reps							
	Weight							
	Reps							
	Weight							

Cardio	Time	Distance	Heart Rate	Cals Burned

Measurements

Neck	R Bicep	L Bicep	Chest	Waist	Hips	R Thigh	L Thigh	Calf

Date:_____ Muscle Group: _____

S M T W T F S   Start Time_____
◯ ◯ ◯ ◯ ◯ ◯ ◯

Weight:_____   Finish Time_____

☐ Upper Body   ☐ Lower Body   ☐ Abs

Exercise	Set	1	2	3	4	5	6	7
	Reps							
	Weight							
	Reps							
	Weight							
	Reps							
	Weight							
	Reps							
	Weight							
	Reps							
	Weight							
	Reps							
	Weight							
	Reps							
	Weight							
	Reps							
	Weight							

Cardio	Time	Distance	Heart Rate	Cals Burned

Measurements

Neck	R Bicep	L Bicep	Chest	Waist	Hips	R Thigh	L Thigh	Calf

Date:_____ **Muscle Group:** _____

S M T W T F S **Start Time**_____
○ ○ ○ ○ ○ ○ ○

Weight:_____ **Finish Time**_____

☐ **Upper Body**   ☐ **Lower Body**   ☐ **Abs**

Exercise	Set	1	2	3	4	5	6	7
	Reps							
	Weight							
	Reps							
	Weight							
	Reps							
	Weight							
	Reps							
	Weight							
	Reps							
	Weight							
	Reps							
	Weight							
	Reps							
	Weight							
	Reps							
	Weight							

Cardio	Time	Distance	Heart Rate	Cals Burned

Measurements

Neck	R Bicep	L Bicep	Chest	Waist	Hips	R Thigh	L Thigh	Calf

Date: _____ **Muscle Group:** _____

S M T W T F S **Start Time** _____
◯ ◯ ◯ ◯ ◯ ◯ ◯

Weight: _____ **Finish Time** _____

☐ **Upper Body**   ☐ **Lower Body**   ☐ **Abs**

Exercise	Set	1	2	3	4	5	6	7
	Reps							
	Weight							
	Reps							
	Weight							
	Reps							
	Weight							
	Reps							
	Weight							
	Reps							
	Weight							
	Reps							
	Weight							
	Reps							
	Weight							
	Reps							
	Weight							

Cardio	Time	Distance	Heart Rate	Cals Burned

Measurements

Neck	R Bicep	L Bicep	Chest	Waist	Hips	R Thigh	L Thigh	Calf

Date:_____ **Muscle Group:** _____

S M T W T F S **Start Time**_____
◯ ◯ ◯ ◯ ◯ ◯ ◯

Weight:_____ **Finish Time**_____

☐ **Upper Body**   ☐ **Lower Body**   ☐ **Abs**

Exercise	Set	1	2	3	4	5	6	7
	Reps							
	Weight							
	Reps							
	Weight							
	Reps							
	Weight							
	Reps							
	Weight							
	Reps							
	Weight							
	Reps							
	Weight							
	Reps							
	Weight							
	Reps							
	Weight							

Cardio	Time	Distance	Heart Rate	Cals Burned

Measurements

Neck	R Bicep	L Bicep	Chest	Waist	Hips	R Thigh	L Thigh	Calf

Date:_____ Muscle Group: _____

S M T W T F S Start Time_____
◯ ◯ ◯ ◯ ◯ ◯ ◯

Weight:_____ Finish Time_____

☐ Upper Body ☐ Lower Body ☐ Abs

Exercise	Set	1	2	3	4	5	6	7
	Reps							
	Weight							
	Reps							
	Weight							
	Reps							
	Weight							
	Reps							
	Weight							
	Reps							
	Weight							
	Reps							
	Weight							
	Reps							
	Weight							
	Reps							
	Weight							

Cardio	Time	Distance	Heart Rate	Cals Burned

Measurements

Neck	R Bicep	L Bicep	Chest	Waist	Hips	R Thigh	L Thigh	Calf

Date:_____ **Muscle Group:** _____

S M T W T F S   **Start Time**_____
◯ ◯ ◯ ◯ ◯ ◯ ◯

Weight:_____   **Finish Time**_____

☐ **Upper Body**   ☐ **Lower Body**   ☐ **Abs**

Exercise	Set	1	2	3	4	5	6	7
	Reps							
	Weight							
	Reps							
	Weight							
	Reps							
	Weight							
	Reps							
	Weight							
	Reps							
	Weight							
	Reps							
	Weight							
	Reps							
	Weight							
	Reps							
	Weight							

Cardio	Time	Distance	Heart Rate	Cals Burned

Measurements

Neck	R Bicep	L Bicep	Chest	Waist	Hips	R Thigh	L Thigh	Calf

Date:_____ **Muscle Group:** _____

S M T W T F S   **Start Time**_____
◯◯◯◯◯◯◯

Weight:_____   **Finish Time**_____

☐ **Upper Body**   ☐ **Lower Body**   ☐ **Abs**

Exercise	Set	1	2	3	4	5	6	7
	Reps							
	Weight							
	Reps							
	Weight							
	Reps							
	Weight							
	Reps							
	Weight							
	Reps							
	Weight							
	Reps							
	Weight							
	Reps							
	Weight							
	Reps							
	Weight							

Cardio	Time	Distance	Heart Rate	Cals Burned

Measurements

Neck	R Bicep	L Bicep	Chest	Waist	Hips	R Thigh	L Thigh	Calf

Date: _____ **Muscle Group:** _____

S M T W T F S
○ ○ ○ ○ ○ ○ ○   **Start Time** _____

Weight: _____ **Finish Time** _____

☐ **Upper Body**   ☐ **Lower Body**   ☐ **Abs**

Exercise	Set	1	2	3	4	5	6	7
	Reps							
	Weight							
	Reps							
	Weight							
	Reps							
	Weight							
	Reps							
	Weight							
	Reps							
	Weight							
	Reps							
	Weight							
	Reps							
	Weight							
	Reps							
	Weight							

Cardio	Time	Distance	Heart Rate	Cals Burned

Measurements

Neck	R Bicep	L Bicep	Chest	Waist	Hips	R Thigh	L Thigh	Calf

Date:_____ **Muscle Group:** _____

S   M   T   W   T   F   S   **Start Time**_____
◯ ◯ ◯ ◯ ◯ ◯ ◯

Weight:_____ **Finish Time**_____

☐ **Upper Body**   ☐ **Lower Body**   ☐ **Abs**

Exercise	Set	1	2	3	4	5	6	7
	Reps							
	Weight							
	Reps							
	Weight							
	Reps							
	Weight							
	Reps							
	Weight							
	Reps							
	Weight							
	Reps							
	Weight							
	Reps							
	Weight							
	Reps							
	Weight							

Cardio	Time	Distance	Heart Rate	Cals Burned

Measurements

Neck	R Bicep	L Bicep	Chest	Waist	Hips	R Thigh	L Thigh	Calf

Date:_____ Muscle Group: _____

S M T W T F S Start Time_____
◯ ◯ ◯ ◯ ◯ ◯ ◯

Weight:_____ Finish Time_____

☐ Upper Body   ☐ Lower Body   ☐ Abs

Exercise	Set	1	2	3	4	5	6	7
	Reps							
	Weight							
	Reps							
	Weight							
	Reps							
	Weight							
	Reps							
	Weight							
	Reps							
	Weight							
	Reps							
	Weight							
	Reps							
	Weight							
	Reps							
	Weight							
	Reps							
	Weight							

Cardio	Time	Distance	Heart Rate	Cals Burned

Measurements

Neck	R Bicep	L Bicep	Chest	Waist	Hips	R Thigh	L Thigh	Calf

Date:_____ **Muscle Group:** _____

S M T W T F S **Start Time**_____
◯ ◯ ◯ ◯ ◯ ◯

Weight:_____ **Finish Time**_____

☐ **Upper Body** ☐ **Lower Body** ☐ **Abs**

Exercise	Set	1	2	3	4	5	6	7
	Reps							
	Weight							
	Reps							
	Weight							
	Reps							
	Weight							
	Reps							
	Weight							
	Reps							
	Weight							
	Reps							
	Weight							
	Reps							
	Weight							
	Reps							
	Weight							

Cardio	Time	Distance	Heart Rate	Cals Burned

Measurements

Neck	R Bicep	L Bicep	Chest	Waist	Hips	R Thigh	L Thigh	Calf

Date:_____ Muscle Group: _____

S M T W T F S   Start Time_____
◯ ◯ ◯ ◯ ◯ ◯ ◯

Weight:_____   Finish Time_____

☐ Upper Body   ☐ Lower Body   ☐ Abs

Exercise	Set	1	2	3	4	5	6	7
	Reps							
	Weight							
	Reps							
	Weight							
	Reps							
	Weight							
	Reps							
	Weight							
	Reps							
	Weight							
	Reps							
	Weight							
	Reps							
	Weight							
	Reps							
	Weight							

Cardio	Time	Distance	Heart Rate	Cals Burned

Measurements

Neck	R Bicep	L Bicep	Chest	Waist	Hips	R Thigh	L Thigh	Calf

Date:_____ Muscle Group: _____

S M T W T F S   Start Time_____
◯ ◯ ◯ ◯ ◯ ◯ ◯

Weight:_____ Finish Time_____

☐ Upper Body   ☐ Lower Body   ☐ Abs

Exercise	Set	1	2	3	4	5	6	7
	Reps							
	Weight							
	Reps							
	Weight							
	Reps							
	Weight							
	Reps							
	Weight							
	Reps							
	Weight							
	Reps							
	Weight							
	Reps							
	Weight							
	Reps							
	Weight							

Cardio	Time	Distance	Heart Rate	Cals Burned

Measurements

Neck	R Bicep	L Bicep	Chest	Waist	Hips	R Thigh	L Thigh	Calf

Date:_____ **Muscle Group:** _____

S M T W T F S **Start Time**_____
◯ ◯ ◯ ◯ ◯ ◯ ◯

Weight:_____ **Finish Time**_____

☐ **Upper Body** ☐ **Lower Body** ☐ **Abs**

Exercise	Set	1	2	3	4	5	6	7
	Reps							
	Weight							
	Reps							
	Weight							
	Reps							
	Weight							
	Reps							
	Weight							
	Reps							
	Weight							
	Reps							
	Weight							
	Reps							
	Weight							
	Reps							
	Weight							

Cardio	Time	Distance	Heart Rate	Cals Burned

Measurements

Neck	R Bicep	L Bicep	Chest	Waist	Hips	R Thigh	L Thigh	Calf

Date:_____ **Muscle Group:** _____

S M T W T F S
○ ○ ○ ○ ○ ○ ○ **Start Time**_____

Weight:_____ **Finish Time**_____

☐ **Upper Body** ☐ **Lower Body** ☐ **Abs**

Exercise	Set	1	2	3	4	5	6	7
	Reps							
	Weight							
	Reps							
	Weight							
	Reps							
	Weight							
	Reps							
	Weight							
	Reps							
	Weight							
	Reps							
	Weight							
	Reps							
	Weight							
	Reps							
	Weight							

Cardio	Time	Distance	Heart Rate	Cals Burned

Measurements

Neck	R Bicep	L Bicep	Chest	Waist	Hips	R Thigh	L Thigh	Calf

Date:_____ **Muscle Group:** _____

S M T W T F S **Start Time**_____
○ ○ ○ ○ ○ ○ ○

Weight:_____ **Finish Time**_____

☐ **Upper Body**   ☐ **Lower Body**   ☐ **Abs**

Exercise	Set	1	2	3	4	5	6	7
	Reps							
	Weight							
	Reps							
	Weight							
	Reps							
	Weight							
	Reps							
	Weight							
	Reps							
	Weight							
	Reps							
	Weight							
	Reps							
	Weight							
	Reps							
	Weight							

Cardio	Time	Distance	Heart Rate	Cals Burned

Measurements

Neck	R Bicep	L Bicep	Chest	Waist	Hips	R Thigh	L Thigh	Calf

Date: _____ **Muscle Group:** _____

S M T W T F S   **Start Time** _____
◯ ◯ ◯ ◯ ◯ ◯ ◯

Weight: _____ **Finish Time** _____

☐ **Upper Body**   ☐ **Lower Body**   ☐ **Abs**

Exercise	Set	1	2	3	4	5	6	7
	Reps							
	Weight							
	Reps							
	Weight							
	Reps							
	Weight							
	Reps							
	Weight							
	Reps							
	Weight							
	Reps							
	Weight							
	Reps							
	Weight							
	Reps							
	Weight							

Cardio	Time	Distance	Heart Rate	Cals Burned

Measurements

Neck	R Bicep	L Bicep	Chest	Waist	Hips	R Thigh	L Thigh	Calf

Date:_____ **Muscle Group:** _____

S M T W T F S **Start Time**_____
○ ○ ○ ○ ○ ○ ○

Weight:_____ **Finish Time**_____

☐ **Upper Body**   ☐ **Lower Body**   ☐ **Abs**

Exercise	Set	1	2	3	4	5	6	7
	Reps							
	Weight							
	Reps							
	Weight							
	Reps							
	Weight							
	Reps							
	Weight							
	Reps							
	Weight							
	Reps							
	Weight							
	Reps							
	Weight							
	Reps							
	Weight							

Cardio	Time	Distance	Heart Rate	Cals Burned

Measurements

Neck	R Bicep	L Bicep	Chest	Waist	Hips	R Thigh	L Thigh	Calf

Date:＿＿＿＿＿＿＿＿   **Muscle Group:** ＿＿＿＿＿＿＿＿

S M T W T F S   **Start Time**＿＿＿＿＿＿＿＿
○ ○ ○ ○ ○ ○ ○

Weight:＿＿＿＿＿＿＿   **Finish Time**＿＿＿＿＿＿＿

☐ **Upper Body**   ☐ **Lower Body**   ☐ **Abs**

Exercise	Set	1	2	3	4	5	6	7
	Reps							
	Weight							
	Reps							
	Weight							
	Reps							
	Weight							
	Reps							
	Weight							
	Reps							
	Weight							
	Reps							
	Weight							
	Reps							
	Weight							
	Reps							
	Weight							

Cardio	Time	Distance	Heart Rate	Cals Burned

Measurements

Neck	R Bicep	L Bicep	Chest	Waist	Hips	R Thigh	L Thigh	Calf

Date:_____ Muscle Group: _____

S M T W T F S   Start Time_____
○ ○ ○ ○ ○ ○ ○

Weight:_____   Finish Time_____

☐ Upper Body   ☐ Lower Body   ☐ Abs

Exercise	Set	1	2	3	4	5	6	7
	Reps							
	Weight							
	Reps							
	Weight							
	Reps							
	Weight							
	Reps							
	Weight							
	Reps							
	Weight							
	Reps							
	Weight							
	Reps							
	Weight							
	Reps							
	Weight							

Cardio	Time	Distance	Heart Rate	Cals Burned

Measurements

Neck	R Bicep	L Bicep	Chest	Waist	Hips	R Thigh	L Thigh	Calf

Date:_____   **Muscle Group:** _____

S   M   T   W   T   F   S   **Start Time**_____
◯   ◯   ◯   ◯   ◯   ◯   ◯

Weight:_____   **Finish Time**_____

☐ **Upper Body**   ☐ **Lower Body**   ☐ **Abs**

Exercise	Set	1	2	3	4	5	6	7
	Reps							
	Weight							
	Reps							
	Weight							
	Reps							
	Weight							
	Reps							
	Weight							
	Reps							
	Weight							
	Reps							
	Weight							
	Reps							
	Weight							
	Reps							
	Weight							

Cardio	Time	Distance	Heart Rate	Cals Burned

Measurements

Neck	R Bicep	L Bicep	Chest	Waist	Hips	R Thigh	L Thigh	Calf

Date:_____ Muscle Group: _____

| S | M | T | W | T | F | S |
| ○ | ○ | ○ | ○ | ○ | ○ | ○ |

Start Time_____

Weight:_____ Finish Time_____

☐ Upper Body   ☐ Lower Body   ☐ Abs

Exercise	Set	1	2	3	4	5	6	7
	Reps							
	Weight							
	Reps							
	Weight							
	Reps							
	Weight							
	Reps							
	Weight							
	Reps							
	Weight							
	Reps							
	Weight							
	Reps							
	Weight							
	Reps							
	Weight							

Cardio	Time	Distance	Heart Rate	Cals Burned

Measurements

Neck	R Bicep	L Bicep	Chest	Waist	Hips	R Thigh	L Thigh	Calf

Date:_____ Muscle Group: _____

S M T W T F S   Start Time_____
○ ○ ○ ○ ○ ○ ○

Weight:_____   Finish Time_____

☐ Upper Body   ☐ Lower Body   ☐ Abs

Exercise	Set	1	2	3	4	5	6	7
	Reps							
	Weight							
	Reps							
	Weight							
	Reps							
	Weight							
	Reps							
	Weight							
	Reps							
	Weight							
	Reps							
	Weight							
	Reps							
	Weight							
	Reps							
	Weight							

Cardio	Time	Distance	Heart Rate	Cals Burned

Measurements

Neck	R Bicep	L Bicep	Chest	Waist	Hips	R Thigh	L Thigh	Calf

Date:_____ Muscle Group: _____

S   M   T   W   T   F   S   Start Time_____
◯   ◯   ◯   ◯   ◯   ◯   ◯

Weight:_____   Finish Time_____

☐ Upper Body   ☐ Lower Body   ☐ Abs

Exercise	Set	1	2	3	4	5	6	7
	Reps							
	Weight							
	Reps							
	Weight							
	Reps							
	Weight							
	Reps							
	Weight							
	Reps							
	Weight							
	Reps							
	Weight							
	Reps							
	Weight							
	Reps							
	Weight							

Cardio	Time	Distance	Heart Rate	Cals Burned

Measurements

Neck	R Bicep	L Bicep	Chest	Waist	Hips	R Thigh	L Thigh	Calf

Date:_____ **Muscle Group:** _____

S M T W T F S **Start Time**_____
◯◯◯◯◯◯◯

Weight:_____ **Finish Time**_____

☐ **Upper Body**   ☐ **Lower Body**   ☐ **Abs**

Exercise	Set	1	2	3	4	5	6	7
	Reps							
	Weight							
	Reps							
	Weight							
	Reps							
	Weight							
	Reps							
	Weight							
	Reps							
	Weight							
	Reps							
	Weight							
	Reps							
	Weight							
	Reps							
	Weight							

Cardio	Time	Distance	Heart Rate	Cals Burned

Measurements

Neck	R Bicep	L Bicep	Chest	Waist	Hips	R Thigh	L Thigh	Calf

Date:_____   Muscle Group: _____

S   M   T   W   T   F   S   Start Time_____
◯   ◯   ◯   ◯   ◯   ◯   ◯

Weight:_____   Finish Time_____

☐ Upper Body   ☐ Lower Body   ☐ Abs

Exercise	Set	1	2	3	4	5	6	7
	Reps							
	Weight							
	Reps							
	Weight							
	Reps							
	Weight							
	Reps							
	Weight							
	Reps							
	Weight							
	Reps							
	Weight							
	Reps							
	Weight							
	Reps							
	Weight							

Cardio	Time	Distance	Heart Rate	Cals Burned

Measurements

Neck	R Bicep	L Bicep	Chest	Waist	Hips	R Thigh	L Thigh	Calf

Date:_____ **Muscle Group:** _____

S   M   T   W   T   F   S   **Start Time**_____
◯ ◯ ◯ ◯ ◯ ◯ ◯

Weight:_____ **Finish Time**_____

☐ **Upper Body**   ☐ **Lower Body**   ☐ **Abs**

Exercise	Set	1	2	3	4	5	6	7
	Reps							
	Weight							
	Reps							
	Weight							
	Reps							
	Weight							
	Reps							
	Weight							
	Reps							
	Weight							
	Reps							
	Weight							
	Reps							
	Weight							
	Reps							
	Weight							

Cardio	Time	Distance	Heart Rate	Cals Burned

Measurements

Neck	R Bicep	L Bicep	Chest	Waist	Hips	R Thigh	L Thigh	Calf

Date:_____   **Muscle Group:** _____

S   M   T   W   T   F   S   **Start Time**_____

◯ ◯ ◯ ◯ ◯ ◯ ◯

Weight:_____   **Finish Time**_____

☐ **Upper Body**   ☐ **Lower Body**   ☐ **Abs**

Exercise	Set	1	2	3	4	5	6	7
	Reps							
	Weight							
	Reps							
	Weight							
	Reps							
	Weight							
	Reps							
	Weight							
	Reps							
	Weight							
	Reps							
	Weight							
	Reps							
	Weight							
	Reps							
	Weight							

Cardio	Time	Distance	Heart Rate	Cals Burned

Measurements

Neck	R Bicep	L Bicep	Chest	Waist	Hips	R Thigh	L Thigh	Calf

Date: _____   **Muscle Group:** _____

S   M   T   W   T   F   S   **Start Time** _____
◯ ◯ ◯ ◯ ◯ ◯ ◯

Weight: _____   **Finish Time** _____

☐ **Upper Body**   ☐ **Lower Body**   ☐ **Abs**

Exercise	Set	1	2	3	4	5	6	7
	Reps							
	Weight							
	Reps							
	Weight							
	Reps							
	Weight							
	Reps							
	Weight							
	Reps							
	Weight							
	Reps							
	Weight							
	Reps							
	Weight							
	Reps							
	Weight							

Cardio	Time	Distance	Heart Rate	Cals Burned

Measurements

Neck	R Bicep	L Bicep	Chest	Waist	Hips	R Thigh	L Thigh	Calf

Date:_____ **Muscle Group:** _____

S M T W T F S **Start Time**_____
◯ ◯ ◯ ◯ ◯ ◯ ◯

Weight:_____ **Finish Time**_____

☐ **Upper Body**   ☐ **Lower Body**   ☐ **Abs**

Exercise	Set	1	2	3	4	5	6	7
	Reps							
	Weight							
	Reps							
	Weight							
	Reps							
	Weight							
	Reps							
	Weight							
	Reps							
	Weight							
	Reps							
	Weight							
	Reps							
	Weight							
	Reps							
	Weight							

Cardio	Time	Distance	Heart Rate	Cals Burned

Measurements

Neck	R Bicep	L Bicep	Chest	Waist	Hips	R Thigh	L Thigh	Calf

Date:_____ **Muscle Group:** _____

S M T W T F S **Start Time**_____
○ ○ ○ ○ ○ ○ ○

Weight:_____ **Finish Time**_____

☐ **Upper Body**   ☐ **Lower Body**   ☐ **Abs**

Exercise	Set	1	2	3	4	5	6	7
	Reps							
	Weight							
	Reps							
	Weight							
	Reps							
	Weight							
	Reps							
	Weight							
	Reps							
	Weight							
	Reps							
	Weight							
	Reps							
	Weight							
	Reps							
	Weight							

Cardio	Time	Distance	Heart Rate	Cals Burned

Measurements

Neck	R Bicep	L Bicep	Chest	Waist	Hips	R Thigh	L Thigh	Calf

Date:_____ Muscle Group: _____

S M T W T F S
◯ ◯ ◯ ◯ ◯ ◯ ◯   Start Time_____

Weight:_____   Finish Time_____

☐ Upper Body   ☐ Lower Body   ☐ Abs

Exercise	Set	1	2	3	4	5	6	7
	Reps							
	Weight							
	Reps							
	Weight							
	Reps							
	Weight							
	Reps							
	Weight							
	Reps							
	Weight							
	Reps							
	Weight							
	Reps							
	Weight							
	Reps							
	Weight							

Cardio	Time	Distance	Heart Rate	Cals Burned

Measurements

Neck	R Bicep	L Bicep	Chest	Waist	Hips	R Thigh	L Thigh	Calf

Date:_____ **Muscle Group:** _____

S M T W T F S   **Start Time**_____
◯ ◯ ◯ ◯ ◯ ◯ ◯

Weight:_____ **Finish Time**_____

☐ **Upper Body**   ☐ **Lower Body**   ☐ **Abs**

Exercise	Set	1	2	3	4	5	6	7
	Reps							
	Weight							
	Reps							
	Weight							
	Reps							
	Weight							
	Reps							
	Weight							
	Reps							
	Weight							
	Reps							
	Weight							
	Reps							
	Weight							
	Reps							
	Weight							

Cardio	Time	Distance	Heart Rate	Cals Burned

Measurements

Neck	R Bicep	L Bicep	Chest	Waist	Hips	R Thigh	L Thigh	Calf

Date:_____ **Muscle Group:** _____

S   M   T   W   T   F   S   **Start Time**_____
◯   ◯   ◯   ◯   ◯   ◯   ◯

Weight:_____ **Finish Time**_____

☐ **Upper Body**   ☐ **Lower Body**   ☐ **Abs**

Exercise	Set	1	2	3	4	5	6	7
	Reps							
	Weight							
	Reps							
	Weight							
	Reps							
	Weight							
	Reps							
	Weight							
	Reps							
	Weight							
	Reps							
	Weight							
	Reps							
	Weight							
	Reps							
	Weight							

Cardio	Time	Distance	Heart Rate	Cals Burned

Measurements

Neck	R Bicep	L Bicep	Chest	Waist	Hips	R Thigh	L Thigh	Calf

Date:_____ Muscle Group: _____

S M T W T F S   **Start Time**_____
◯◯◯◯◯◯◯

Weight:_____   Finish Time_____

☐ **Upper Body**   ☐ **Lower Body**   ☐ **Abs**

Exercise	Set	1	2	3	4	5	6	7
	Reps							
	Weight							
	Reps							
	Weight							
	Reps							
	Weight							
	Reps							
	Weight							
	Reps							
	Weight							
	Reps							
	Weight							
	Reps							
	Weight							
	Reps							
	Weight							

Cardio	Time	Distance	Heart Rate	Cals Burned

Measurements

Neck	R Bicep	L Bicep	Chest	Waist	Hips	R Thigh	L Thigh	Calf

Date:_____ **Muscle Group:** _____

S M T W T F S **Start Time**_____

◯ ◯ ◯ ◯ ◯ ◯ ◯

Weight:_____ **Finish Time**_____

☐ **Upper Body**   ☐ **Lower Body**   ☐ **Abs**

Exercise	Set	1	2	3	4	5	6	7
	Reps							
	Weight							
	Reps							
	Weight							
	Reps							
	Weight							
	Reps							
	Weight							
	Reps							
	Weight							
	Reps							
	Weight							
	Reps							
	Weight							
	Reps							
	Weight							

Cardio	Time	Distance	Heart Rate	Cals Burned

Measurements

Neck	R Bicep	L Bicep	Chest	Waist	Hips	R Thigh	L Thigh	Calf

Date:_____ **Muscle Group:** _____

S M T W T F S **Start Time**_____
◯ ◯ ◯ ◯ ◯ ◯ ◯

Weight:_____ **Finish Time**_____

☐ **Upper Body**   ☐ **Lower Body**   ☐ **Abs**

Exercise	Set	1	2	3	4	5	6	7
	Reps							
	Weight							
	Reps							
	Weight							
	Reps							
	Weight							
	Reps							
	Weight							
	Reps							
	Weight							
	Reps							
	Weight							
	Reps							
	Weight							
	Reps							
	Weight							

Cardio	Time	Distance	Heart Rate	Cals Burned

Measurements

Neck	R Bicep	L Bicep	Chest	Waist	Hips	R Thigh	L Thigh	Calf

Date: _____ **Muscle Group:** _____

S   M   T   W   T   F   S   **Start Time** _____
◯   ◯   ◯   ◯   ◯   ◯   ◯

Weight: _____ **Finish Time** _____

☐ **Upper Body**   ☐ **Lower Body**   ☐ **Abs**

Exercise	Set	1	2	3	4	5	6	7
	Reps							
	Weight							
	Reps							
	Weight							
	Reps							
	Weight							
	Reps							
	Weight							
	Reps							
	Weight							
	Reps							
	Weight							
	Reps							
	Weight							
	Reps							
	Weight							

Cardio	Time	Distance	Heart Rate	Cals Burned

Measurements

Neck	R Bicep	L Bicep	Chest	Waist	Hips	R Thigh	L Thigh	Calf

Date:_____   **Muscle Group:** _____

S M T W T F S   **Start Time**_____
◯ ◯ ◯ ◯ ◯ ◯ ◯

Weight:_____   **Finish Time**_____

☐ **Upper Body**   ☐ **Lower Body**   ☐ **Abs**

Exercise	Set	1	2	3	4	5	6	7
	Reps							
	Weight							
	Reps							
	Weight							
	Reps							
	Weight							
	Reps							
	Weight							
	Reps							
	Weight							
	Reps							
	Weight							
	Reps							
	Weight							
	Reps							
	Weight							

Cardio	Time	Distance	Heart Rate	Cals Burned

Measurements

Neck	R Bicep	L Bicep	Chest	Waist	Hips	R Thigh	L Thigh	Calf

Date:_____ Muscle Group: _____

S M T W T F S Start Time_____
◯ ◯ ◯ ◯ ◯ ◯ ◯

Weight:_____ Finish Time_____

☐ Upper Body ☐ Lower Body ☐ Abs

Exercise	Set	1	2	3	4	5	6	7
	Reps							
	Weight							
	Reps							
	Weight							
	Reps							
	Weight							
	Reps							
	Weight							
	Reps							
	Weight							
	Reps							
	Weight							
	Reps							
	Weight							
	Reps							
	Weight							

Cardio	Time	Distance	Heart Rate	Cals Burned

Measurements

Neck	R Bicep	L Bicep	Chest	Waist	Hips	R Thigh	L Thigh	Calf

Date:_____ Muscle Group: _____

S M T W T F S
○ ○ ○ ○ ○ ○ ○

Start Time_____

Weight:_____

Finish Time_____

☐ Upper Body   ☐ Lower Body   ☐ Abs

Exercise	Set	1	2	3	4	5	6	7
	Reps							
	Weight							
	Reps							
	Weight							
	Reps							
	Weight							
	Reps							
	Weight							
	Reps							
	Weight							
	Reps							
	Weight							
	Reps							
	Weight							
	Reps							
	Weight							

Cardio	Time	Distance	Heart Rate	Cals Burned

Measurements

Neck	R Bicep	L Bicep	Chest	Waist	Hips	R Thigh	L Thigh	Calf

Date:_____ **Muscle Group:** _____

S M T W T F S   **Start Time**_____
◯ ◯ ◯ ◯ ◯ ◯ ◯

Weight:_____   **Finish Time**_____

☐ **Upper Body**   ☐ **Lower Body**   ☐ **Abs**

Exercise	Set	1	2	3	4	5	6	7
	Reps							
	Weight							
	Reps							
	Weight							
	Reps							
	Weight							
	Reps							
	Weight							
	Reps							
	Weight							
	Reps							
	Weight							
	Reps							
	Weight							
	Reps							
	Weight							

Cardio	Time	Distance	Heart Rate	Cals Burned

Measurements

Neck	R Bicep	L Bicep	Chest	Waist	Hips	R Thigh	L Thigh	Calf

Date:_____ Muscle Group: _____

S M T W T F S   Start Time_____
◯ ◯ ◯ ◯ ◯ ◯ ◯

Weight:_____   Finish Time_____

☐ Upper Body   ☐ Lower Body   ☐ Abs

Exercise	Set	1	2	3	4	5	6	7
	Reps							
	Weight							
	Reps							
	Weight							
	Reps							
	Weight							
	Reps							
	Weight							
	Reps							
	Weight							
	Reps							
	Weight							
	Reps							
	Weight							
	Reps							
	Weight							

Cardio	Time	Distance	Heart Rate	Cals Burned

Measurements

Neck	R Bicep	L Bicep	Chest	Waist	Hips	R Thigh	L Thigh	Calf

Date:_____ Muscle Group: _____

S M T W T F S Start Time_____
◯ ◯ ◯ ◯ ◯ ◯ ◯

Weight:_____ Finish Time_____

☐ Upper Body   ☐ Lower Body   ☐ Abs

Exercise	Set	1	2	3	4	5	6	7
	Reps							
	Weight							
	Reps							
	Weight							
	Reps							
	Weight							
	Reps							
	Weight							
	Reps							
	Weight							
	Reps							
	Weight							
	Reps							
	Weight							
	Reps							
	Weight							

Cardio	Time	Distance	Heart Rate	Cals Burned

Measurements

Neck	R Bicep	L Bicep	Chest	Waist	Hips	R Thigh	L Thigh	Calf

Date:_____ Muscle Group: _____

S M T W T F S Start Time_____
◯ ◯ ◯ ◯ ◯ ◯ ◯

Weight:_____ Finish Time_____

☐ Upper Body   ☐ Lower Body   ☐ Abs

Exercise	Set	1	2	3	4	5	6	7
	Reps							
	Weight							
	Reps							
	Weight							
	Reps							
	Weight							
	Reps							
	Weight							
	Reps							
	Weight							
	Reps							
	Weight							
	Reps							
	Weight							
	Reps							
	Weight							

Cardio	Time	Distance	Heart Rate	Cals Burned

Measurements

Neck	R Bicep	L Bicep	Chest	Waist	Hips	R Thigh	L Thigh	Calf

Date:_____ Muscle Group: _____

S M T W T F S
◯ ◯ ◯ ◯ ◯ ◯ ◯

Start Time _____

Weight:_____

Finish Time _____

☐ Upper Body   ☐ Lower Body   ☐ Abs

Exercise	Set	1	2	3	4	5	6	7
	Reps							
	Weight							
	Reps							
	Weight							
	Reps							
	Weight							
	Reps							
	Weight							
	Reps							
	Weight							
	Reps							
	Weight							
	Reps							
	Weight							
	Reps							
	Weight							

Cardio	Time	Distance	Heart Rate	Cals Burned

Measurements

Neck	R Bicep	L Bicep	Chest	Waist	Hips	R Thigh	L Thigh	Calf

Date:_____   **Muscle Group:** _____

S M T W T F S   **Start Time**_____
○ ○ ○ ○ ○ ○ ○

Weight:_____   **Finish Time**_____

☐ **Upper Body**   ☐ **Lower Body**   ☐ **Abs**

Exercise	Set	1	2	3	4	5	6	7
	Reps							
	Weight							
	Reps							
	Weight							
	Reps							
	Weight							
	Reps							
	Weight							
	Reps							
	Weight							
	Reps							
	Weight							
	Reps							
	Weight							
	Reps							
	Weight							

Cardio	Time	Distance	Heart Rate	Cals Burned

Measurements

Neck	R Bicep	L Bicep	Chest	Waist	Hips	R Thigh	L Thigh	Calf

Date:＿＿＿＿＿＿＿＿＿ **Muscle Group:** ＿＿＿＿＿＿＿＿

S M T W T F S
◯ ◯ ◯ ◯ ◯ ◯ ◯   **Start Time**＿＿＿＿＿＿＿＿＿

Weight:＿＿＿＿＿＿＿＿＿   **Finish Time**＿＿＿＿＿＿＿＿＿

☐ **Upper Body**   ☐ **Lower Body**   ☐ **Abs**

Exercise	Set	1	2	3	4	5	6	7
	Reps							
	Weight							
	Reps							
	Weight							
	Reps							
	Weight							
	Reps							
	Weight							
	Reps							
	Weight							
	Reps							
	Weight							
	Reps							
	Weight							
	Reps							
	Weight							

Cardio	Time	Distance	Heart Rate	Cals Burned

Measurements

Neck	R Bicep	L Bicep	Chest	Waist	Hips	R Thigh	L Thigh	Calf

Date:_____ **Muscle Group:** _____

S M T W T F S **Start Time**_____
◯ ◯ ◯ ◯ ◯ ◯ ◯

Weight:_____ **Finish Time**_____

☐ Upper Body ☐ Lower Body ☐ Abs

Exercise	Set	1	2	3	4	5	6	7
	Reps							
	Weight							
	Reps							
	Weight							
	Reps							
	Weight							
	Reps							
	Weight							
	Reps							
	Weight							
	Reps							
	Weight							
	Reps							
	Weight							
	Reps							
	Weight							

Cardio	Time	Distance	Heart Rate	Cals Burned

Measurements

Neck	R Bicep	L Bicep	Chest	Waist	Hips	R Thigh	L Thigh	Calf

Date:_____ **Muscle Group:** _____

S M T W T F S   **Start Time**_____
○ ○ ○ ○ ○ ○ ○

Weight:_____ **Finish Time**_____

☐ **Upper Body**   ☐ **Lower Body**   ☐ **Abs**

Exercise	Set	1	2	3	4	5	6	7
	Reps							
	Weight							
	Reps							
	Weight							
	Reps							
	Weight							
	Reps							
	Weight							
	Reps							
	Weight							
	Reps							
	Weight							
	Reps							
	Weight							
	Reps							
	Weight							

Cardio	Time	Distance	Heart Rate	Cals Burned

Measurements

Neck	R Bicep	L Bicep	Chest	Waist	Hips	R Thigh	L Thigh	Calf

Date:_____ **Muscle Group:** _____

S M T W T F S **Start Time**_____
◯ ◯ ◯ ◯ ◯ ◯ ◯

Weight:_____ **Finish Time**_____

☐ **Upper Body**   ☐ **Lower Body**   ☐ **Abs**

Exercise	Set	1	2	3	4	5	6	7
	Reps							
	Weight							
	Reps							
	Weight							
	Reps							
	Weight							
	Reps							
	Weight							
	Reps							
	Weight							
	Reps							
	Weight							
	Reps							
	Weight							
	Reps							
	Weight							

Cardio	Time	Distance	Heart Rate	Cals Burned

Measurements

Neck	R Bicep	L Bicep	Chest	Waist	Hips	R Thigh	L Thigh	Calf

Date:_____ **Muscle Group:** _____

S M T W T F S **Start Time**_____
○ ○ ○ ○ ○ ○ ○

Weight:_____ **Finish Time**_____

☐ **Upper Body**   ☐ **Lower Body**   ☐ **Abs**

Exercise	Set	1	2	3	4	5	6	7
	Reps							
	Weight							
	Reps							
	Weight							
	Reps							
	Weight							
	Reps							
	Weight							
	Reps							
	Weight							
	Reps							
	Weight							
	Reps							
	Weight							
	Reps							
	Weight							

Cardio	Time	Distance	Heart Rate	Cals Burned

Measurements

Neck	R Bicep	L Bicep	Chest	Waist	Hips	R Thigh	L Thigh	Calf

Date:_____ **Muscle Group:** _____

S	M	T	W	T	F	S
○	○	○	○	○	○	○

Start Time_____

Weight:_____ **Finish Time**_____

☐ **Upper Body**   ☐ **Lower Body**   ☐ **Abs**

Exercise	Set	1	2	3	4	5	6	7
	Reps							
	Weight							
	Reps							
	Weight							
	Reps							
	Weight							
	Reps							
	Weight							
	Reps							
	Weight							
	Reps							
	Weight							
	Reps							
	Weight							
	Reps							
	Weight							

Cardio	Time	Distance	Heart Rate	Cals Burned

Measurements

Neck	R Bicep	L Bicep	Chest	Waist	Hips	R Thigh	L Thigh	Calf

Date:_____   Muscle Group: _____

S   M   T   W   T   F   S   Start Time_____
◯   ◯   ◯   ◯   ◯   ◯   ◯

Weight:_____   Finish Time_____

☐ Upper Body   ☐ Lower Body   ☐ Abs

Exercise	Set	1	2	3	4	5	6	7
	Reps							
	Weight							
	Reps							
	Weight							
	Reps							
	Weight							
	Reps							
	Weight							
	Reps							
	Weight							
	Reps							
	Weight							
	Reps							
	Weight							
	Reps							
	Weight							

Cardio	Time	Distance	Heart Rate	Cals Burned

Measurements

Neck	R Bicep	L Bicep	Chest	Waist	Hips	R Thigh	L Thigh	Calf

Date:_____ Muscle Group: _____

S M T W T F S Start Time_____
○ ○ ○ ○ ○ ○ ○

Weight:_____ Finish Time_____

☐ Upper Body ☐ Lower Body ☐ Abs

Exercise	Set	1	2	3	4	5	6	7
	Reps							
	Weight							
	Reps							
	Weight							
	Reps							
	Weight							
	Reps							
	Weight							
	Reps							
	Weight							
	Reps							
	Weight							
	Reps							
	Weight							
	Reps							
	Weight							

Cardio	Time	Distance	Heart Rate	Cals Burned

Measurements

Neck	R Bicep	L Bicep	Chest	Waist	Hips	R Thigh	L Thigh	Calf

Date:_____ Muscle Group: _____

S M T W T F S Start Time_____
◯ ◯ ◯ ◯ ◯ ◯ ◯
Weight:_____ Finish Time_____

☐ Upper Body ☐ Lower Body ☐ Abs

Exercise	Set	1	2	3	4	5	6	7
	Reps							
	Weight							
	Reps							
	Weight							
	Reps							
	Weight							
	Reps							
	Weight							
	Reps							
	Weight							
	Reps							
	Weight							
	Reps							
	Weight							
	Reps							
	Weight							

Cardio	Time	Distance	Heart Rate	Cals Burned

Measurements

Neck	R Bicep	L Bicep	Chest	Waist	Hips	R Thigh	L Thigh	Calf

Date:_____ **Muscle Group:** _____

S M T W T F S **Start Time**_____
◯◯◯◯◯◯◯

Weight:_____ **Finish Time**_____

☐ **Upper Body** ☐ **Lower Body** ☐ **Abs**

Exercise	Set	1	2	3	4	5	6	7
	Reps							
	Weight							
	Reps							
	Weight							
	Reps							
	Weight							
	Reps							
	Weight							
	Reps							
	Weight							
	Reps							
	Weight							
	Reps							
	Weight							
	Reps							
	Weight							

Cardio	Time	Distance	Heart Rate	Cals Burned

Measurements

Neck	R Bicep	L Bicep	Chest	Waist	Hips	R Thigh	L Thigh	Calf

Date:_____ **Muscle Group:** _____

S M T W T F S   **Start Time**_____
◯ ◯ ◯ ◯ ◯ ◯ ◯

Weight:_____ **Finish Time**_____

☐ **Upper Body**   ☐ **Lower Body**   ☐ **Abs**

Exercise	Set	1	2	3	4	5	6	7
	Reps							
	Weight							
	Reps							
	Weight							
	Reps							
	Weight							
	Reps							
	Weight							
	Reps							
	Weight							
	Reps							
	Weight							
	Reps							
	Weight							
	Reps							
	Weight							

Cardio	Time	Distance	Heart Rate	Cals Burned

Measurements

Neck	R Bicep	L Bicep	Chest	Waist	Hips	R Thigh	L Thigh	Calf

Date:_____ **Muscle Group:** _____

S M T W T F S **Start Time**_____
○ ○ ○ ○ ○ ○ ○

Weight:_____ **Finish Time**_____

☐ **Upper Body**   ☐ **Lower Body**   ☐ **Abs**

Exercise	Set	1	2	3	4	5	6	7
	Reps							
	Weight							
	Reps							
	Weight							
	Reps							
	Weight							
	Reps							
	Weight							
	Reps							
	Weight							
	Reps							
	Weight							
	Reps							
	Weight							
	Reps							
	Weight							

Cardio	Time	Distance	Heart Rate	Cals Burned

Measurements

Neck	R Bicep	L Bicep	Chest	Waist	Hips	R Thigh	L Thigh	Calf

Date:_____   **Muscle Group:** _____

S M T W T F S   **Start Time**_____
◯ ◯ ◯ ◯ ◯ ◯ ◯

Weight:_____   **Finish Time**_____

☐ **Upper Body**   ☐ **Lower Body**   ☐ **Abs**

Exercise	Set	1	2	3	4	5	6	7
	Reps							
	Weight							
	Reps							
	Weight							
	Reps							
	Weight							
	Reps							
	Weight							
	Reps							
	Weight							
	Reps							
	Weight							
	Reps							
	Weight							
	Reps							
	Weight							

Cardio	Time	Distance	Heart Rate	Cals Burned

Measurements

Neck	R Bicep	L Bicep	Chest	Waist	Hips	R Thigh	L Thigh	Calf

Date:_____ Muscle Group: _____

S M T W T F S   Start Time_____
○ ○ ○ ○ ○ ○ ○

Weight:_____   Finish Time_____

☐ Upper Body   ☐ Lower Body   ☐ Abs

Exercise	Set	1	2	3	4	5	6	7
	Reps							
	Weight							
	Reps							
	Weight							
	Reps							
	Weight							
	Reps							
	Weight							
	Reps							
	Weight							
	Reps							
	Weight							
	Reps							
	Weight							
	Reps							
	Weight							

Cardio	Time	Distance	Heart Rate	Cals Burned

Measurements

Neck	R Bicep	L Bicep	Chest	Waist	Hips	R Thigh	L Thigh	Calf

Date:_____   **Muscle Group:** _____

S M T W T F S   **Start Time**_____
◯ ◯ ◯ ◯ ◯ ◯ ◯

Weight:_____   **Finish Time**_____

☐ **Upper Body**   ☐ **Lower Body**   ☐ **Abs**

Exercise	Set	1	2	3	4	5	6	7
	Reps							
	Weight							
	Reps							
	Weight							
	Reps							
	Weight							
	Reps							
	Weight							
	Reps							
	Weight							
	Reps							
	Weight							
	Reps							
	Weight							
	Reps							
	Weight							

Cardio	Time	Distance	Heart Rate	Cals Burned

Measurements

Neck	R Bicep	L Bicep	Chest	Waist	Hips	R Thigh	L Thigh	Calf

Date:_____   **Muscle Group:** _____

S M T W T F S   **Start Time**_____
◯ ◯ ◯ ◯ ◯ ◯ ◯

Weight:_____   **Finish Time**_____

☐ **Upper Body**   ☐ **Lower Body**   ☐ **Abs**

Exercise	Set	1	2	3	4	5	6	7
	Reps							
	Weight							
	Reps							
	Weight							
	Reps							
	Weight							
	Reps							
	Weight							
	Reps							
	Weight							
	Reps							
	Weight							
	Reps							
	Weight							
	Reps							
	Weight							

Cardio	Time	Distance	Heart Rate	Cals Burned

Measurements

Neck	R Bicep	L Bicep	Chest	Waist	Hips	R Thigh	L Thigh	Calf

Date:_____ Muscle Group: _____

S M T W T F S   Start Time_____
○ ○ ○ ○ ○ ○ ○

Weight:_____ Finish Time_____

☐ Upper Body   ☐ Lower Body   ☐ Abs

Exercise	Set	1	2	3	4	5	6	7
	Reps							
	Weight							
	Reps							
	Weight							
	Reps							
	Weight							
	Reps							
	Weight							
	Reps							
	Weight							
	Reps							
	Weight							
	Reps							
	Weight							
	Reps							
	Weight							

Cardio	Time	Distance	Heart Rate	Cals Burned

Measurements

Neck	R Bicep	L Bicep	Chest	Waist	Hips	R Thigh	L Thigh	Calf

Date:_____   **Muscle Group:** _____

S   M   T   W   T   F   S   **Start Time**_____
○ ○ ○ ○ ○ ○ ○

Weight:_____   **Finish Time**_____

☐ **Upper Body**   ☐ **Lower Body**   ☐ **Abs**

Exercise	Set	1	2	3	4	5	6	7
	Reps							
	Weight							
	Reps							
	Weight							
	Reps							
	Weight							
	Reps							
	Weight							
	Reps							
	Weight							
	Reps							
	Weight							
	Reps							
	Weight							
	Reps							
	Weight							

Cardio	Time	Distance	Heart Rate	Cals Burned

Measurements

Neck	R Bicep	L Bicep	Chest	Waist	Hips	R Thigh	L Thigh	Calf

Date:_____ **Muscle Group:** _____

S M T W T F S   **Start Time**_____
◯ ◯ ◯ ◯ ◯ ◯ ◯

Weight:_____   **Finish Time**_____

☐ **Upper Body**   ☐ **Lower Body**   ☐ **Abs**

Exercise	Set	1	2	3	4	5	6	7
	Reps							
	Weight							
	Reps							
	Weight							
	Reps							
	Weight							
	Reps							
	Weight							
	Reps							
	Weight							
	Reps							
	Weight							
	Reps							
	Weight							
	Reps							
	Weight							

Cardio	Time	Distance	Heart Rate	Cals Burned

Measurements

Neck	R Bicep	L Bicep	Chest	Waist	Hips	R Thigh	L Thigh	Calf

Date:_____ **Muscle Group:** _____

S   M   T   W   T   F   S   **Start Time**_____
◯ ◯ ◯ ◯ ◯ ◯ ◯

Weight:_____ **Finish Time**_____

☐ **Upper Body**   ☐ **Lower Body**   ☐ **Abs**

Exercise	Set	1	2	3	4	5	6	7
	Reps							
	Weight							
	Reps							
	Weight							
	Reps							
	Weight							
	Reps							
	Weight							
	Reps							
	Weight							
	Reps							
	Weight							
	Reps							
	Weight							
	Reps							
	Weight							

Cardio	Time	Distance	Heart Rate	Cals Burned

Measurements

Neck	R Bicep	L Bicep	Chest	Waist	Hips	R Thigh	L Thigh	Calf

Date:_____ **Muscle Group:** _____

S M T W T F S
◯ ◯ ◯ ◯ ◯ ◯ ◯

Start Time_____

Weight:_____ **Finish Time**_____

☐ **Upper Body**   ☐ **Lower Body**   ☐ **Abs**

Exercise	Set	1	2	3	4	5	6	7
	Reps							
	Weight							
	Reps							
	Weight							
	Reps							
	Weight							
	Reps							
	Weight							
	Reps							
	Weight							
	Reps							
	Weight							
	Reps							
	Weight							
	Reps							
	Weight							

Cardio	Time	Distance	Heart Rate	Cals Burned

Measurements

Neck	R Bicep	L Bicep	Chest	Waist	Hips	R Thigh	L Thigh	Calf

Date:_____ **Muscle Group:** _____

S	M	T	W	T	F	S
◯	◯	◯	◯	◯	◯	◯

Start Time_____

Weight:_____ **Finish Time**_____

☐ **Upper Body**   ☐ **Lower Body**   ☐ **Abs**

Exercise	Set	1	2	3	4	5	6	7
	Reps							
	Weight							
	Reps							
	Weight							
	Reps							
	Weight							
	Reps							
	Weight							
	Reps							
	Weight							
	Reps							
	Weight							
	Reps							
	Weight							
	Reps							
	Weight							

Cardio	Time	Distance	Heart Rate	Cals Burned

Measurements

Neck	R Bicep	L Bicep	Chest	Waist	Hips	R Thigh	L Thigh	Calf

Date:_____ Muscle Group: _____

S M T W T F S Start Time_____
◯ ◯ ◯ ◯ ◯ ◯ ◯

Weight:_____ Finish Time_____

☐ Upper Body   ☐ Lower Body   ☐ Abs

Exercise	Set	1	2	3	4	5	6	7
	Reps							
	Weight							
	Reps							
	Weight							
	Reps							
	Weight							
	Reps							
	Weight							
	Reps							
	Weight							
	Reps							
	Weight							
	Reps							
	Weight							
	Reps							
	Weight							

Cardio	Time	Distance	Heart Rate	Cals Burned

Measurements

Neck	R Bicep	L Bicep	Chest	Waist	Hips	R Thigh	L Thigh	Calf

Date:_____ Muscle Group: _____

S M T W T F S
○ ○ ○ ○ ○ ○ ○

Start Time_____

Weight:_____

Finish Time_____

☐ Upper Body   ☐ Lower Body   ☐ Abs

Exercise	Set	1	2	3	4	5	6	7
	Reps							
	Weight							
	Reps							
	Weight							
	Reps							
	Weight							
	Reps							
	Weight							
	Reps							
	Weight							
	Reps							
	Weight							
	Reps							
	Weight							
	Reps							
	Weight							

Cardio	Time	Distance	Heart Rate	Cals Burned

Measurements

Neck	R Bicep	L Bicep	Chest	Waist	Hips	R Thigh	L Thigh	Calf

Date:_____ Muscle Group: _____

S M T W T F S   Start Time_____
○ ○ ○ ○ ○ ○ ○

Weight:_____   Finish Time_____

☐ Upper Body   ☐ Lower Body   ☐ Abs

Exercise	Set	1	2	3	4	5	6	7
	Reps							
	Weight							
	Reps							
	Weight							
	Reps							
	Weight							
	Reps							
	Weight							
	Reps							
	Weight							
	Reps							
	Weight							
	Reps							
	Weight							
	Reps							
	Weight							

Cardio	Time	Distance	Heart Rate	Cals Burned

Measurements

Neck	R Bicep	L Bicep	Chest	Waist	Hips	R Thigh	L Thigh	Calf

Date:_____   Muscle Group: _____

S M T W T F S   Start Time_____
◯ ◯ ◯ ◯ ◯ ◯ ◯

Weight:_____   Finish Time_____

☐ Upper Body   ☐ Lower Body   ☐ Abs

Exercise	Set	1	2	3	4	5	6	7
	Reps							
	Weight							
	Reps							
	Weight							
	Reps							
	Weight							
	Reps							
	Weight							
	Reps							
	Weight							
	Reps							
	Weight							
	Reps							
	Weight							
	Reps							
	Weight							

Cardio	Time	Distance	Heart Rate	Cals Burned

Measurements

Neck	R Bicep	L Bicep	Chest	Waist	Hips	R Thigh	L Thigh	Calf

Date: _____ **Muscle Group:** _____

S M T W T F S **Start Time** _____
◯ ◯ ◯ ◯ ◯ ◯ ◯

Weight: _____ **Finish Time** _____

☐ **Upper Body**   ☐ **Lower Body**   ☐ **Abs**

Exercise	Set	1	2	3	4	5	6	7
	Reps							
	Weight							
	Reps							
	Weight							
	Reps							
	Weight							
	Reps							
	Weight							
	Reps							
	Weight							
	Reps							
	Weight							
	Reps							
	Weight							
	Reps							
	Weight							

Cardio	Time	Distance	Heart Rate	Cals Burned

Measurements

Neck	R Bicep	L Bicep	Chest	Waist	Hips	R Thigh	L Thigh	Calf

Date:_____ **Muscle Group:** _____

S M T W T F S **Start Time**_____
〇 〇 〇 〇 〇 〇 〇

Weight:_____ **Finish Time**_____

☐ **Upper Body**   ☐ **Lower Body**   ☐ **Abs**

Exercise	Set	1	2	3	4	5	6	7
	Reps							
	Weight							
	Reps							
	Weight							
	Reps							
	Weight							
	Reps							
	Weight							
	Reps							
	Weight							
	Reps							
	Weight							
	Reps							
	Weight							
	Reps							
	Weight							

Cardio	Time	Distance	Heart Rate	Cals Burned

Measurements

Neck	R Bicep	L Bicep	Chest	Waist	Hips	R Thigh	L Thigh	Calf

Date:_____ **Muscle Group:** _____

S M T W T F S **Start Time**_____
◯ ◯ ◯ ◯ ◯ ◯ ◯

Weight:_____ **Finish Time**_____

☐ **Upper Body** ☐ **Lower Body** ☐ **Abs**

Exercise	Set	1	2	3	4	5	6	7
	Reps							
	Weight							
	Reps							
	Weight							
	Reps							
	Weight							
	Reps							
	Weight							
	Reps							
	Weight							
	Reps							
	Weight							
	Reps							
	Weight							
	Reps							
	Weight							

Cardio	Time	Distance	Heart Rate	Cals Burned

Measurements

Neck	R Bicep	L Bicep	Chest	Waist	Hips	R Thigh	L Thigh	Calf

Date: _____ **Muscle Group:** _____

S M T W T F S **Start Time** _____
○ ○ ○ ○ ○ ○ ○

Weight: _____ **Finish Time** _____

☐ **Upper Body**   ☐ **Lower Body**   ☐ **Abs**

Exercise	Set	1	2	3	4	5	6	7
	Reps							
	Weight							
	Reps							
	Weight							
	Reps							
	Weight							
	Reps							
	Weight							
	Reps							
	Weight							
	Reps							
	Weight							
	Reps							
	Weight							
	Reps							
	Weight							

Cardio	Time	Distance	Heart Rate	Cals Burned

Measurements

Neck	R Bicep	L Bicep	Chest	Waist	Hips	R Thigh	L Thigh	Calf

Date:_____ **Muscle Group:** _____

S M T W T F S **Start Time**_____
◯ ◯ ◯ ◯ ◯ ◯ ◯

Weight:_____ **Finish Time**_____

☐ **Upper Body**   ☐ **Lower Body**   ☐ **Abs**

Exercise	Set	1	2	3	4	5	6	7
	Reps							
	Weight							
	Reps							
	Weight							
	Reps							
	Weight							
	Reps							
	Weight							
	Reps							
	Weight							
	Reps							
	Weight							
	Reps							
	Weight							
	Reps							
	Weight							

Cardio	Time	Distance	Heart Rate	Cals Burned

Measurements

Neck	R Bicep	L Bicep	Chest	Waist	Hips	R Thigh	L Thigh	Calf

Date:_____   **Muscle Group:** _____

S M T W T F S   **Start Time**_____
〇 〇 〇 〇 〇 〇 〇

Weight:_____   **Finish Time**_____

☐ **Upper Body**   ☐ **Lower Body**   ☐ **Abs**

Exercise	Set	1	2	3	4	5	6	7
	Reps							
	Weight							
	Reps							
	Weight							
	Reps							
	Weight							
	Reps							
	Weight							
	Reps							
	Weight							
	Reps							
	Weight							
	Reps							
	Weight							
	Reps							
	Weight							

Cardio	Time	Distance	Heart Rate	Cals Burned

Measurements

Neck	R Bicep	L Bicep	Chest	Waist	Hips	R Thigh	L Thigh	Calf

Date:_____ Muscle Group: _____

S M T W T F S
◯ ◯ ◯ ◯ ◯ ◯ ◯

Start Time_____

Weight:_____

Finish Time_____

☐ Upper Body   ☐ Lower Body   ☐ Abs

Exercise	Set	1	2	3	4	5	6	7
	Reps							
	Weight							
	Reps							
	Weight							
	Reps							
	Weight							
	Reps							
	Weight							
	Reps							
	Weight							
	Reps							
	Weight							
	Reps							
	Weight							
	Reps							
	Weight							

Cardio	Time	Distance	Heart Rate	Cals Burned

Measurements

Neck	R Bicep	L Bicep	Chest	Waist	Hips	R Thigh	L Thigh	Calf

Date:_____   **Muscle Group:** _____

S   M   T   W   T   F   S   **Start Time**_____
◯   ◯   ◯   ◯   ◯   ◯   ◯

Weight:_____   **Finish Time**_____

☐ **Upper Body**   ☐ **Lower Body**   ☐ **Abs**

Exercise	Set	1	2	3	4	5	6	7
	Reps							
	Weight							
	Reps							
	Weight							
	Reps							
	Weight							
	Reps							
	Weight							
	Reps							
	Weight							
	Reps							
	Weight							
	Reps							
	Weight							
	Reps							
	Weight							

Cardio	Time	Distance	Heart Rate	Cals Burned

Measurements

Neck	R Bicep	L Bicep	Chest	Waist	Hips	R Thigh	L Thigh	Calf

Date:_____ Muscle Group: _____

S M T W T F S   Start Time_____
◯ ◯ ◯ ◯ ◯ ◯ ◯

Weight:_____ Finish Time_____

☐ Upper Body   ☐ Lower Body   ☐ Abs

Exercise	Set	1	2	3	4	5	6	7
	Reps							
	Weight							
	Reps							
	Weight							
	Reps							
	Weight							
	Reps							
	Weight							
	Reps							
	Weight							
	Reps							
	Weight							
	Reps							
	Weight							
	Reps							
	Weight							

Cardio	Time	Distance	Heart Rate	Cals Burned

Measurements

Neck	R Bicep	L Bicep	Chest	Waist	Hips	R Thigh	L Thigh	Calf

Date:_____ **Muscle Group:** _____

S M T W T F S   **Start Time**_____
◯ ◯ ◯ ◯ ◯ ◯ ◯

Weight:_____   **Finish Time**_____

☐ **Upper Body**   ☐ **Lower Body**   ☐ **Abs**

Exercise	Set	1	2	3	4	5	6	7
	Reps							
	Weight							
	Reps							
	Weight							
	Reps							
	Weight							
	Reps							
	Weight							
	Reps							
	Weight							
	Reps							
	Weight							
	Reps							
	Weight							
	Reps							
	Weight							

Cardio	Time	Distance	Heart Rate	Cals Burned

Measurements

Neck	R Bicep	L Bicep	Chest	Waist	Hips	R Thigh	L Thigh	Calf

Date:_____ **Muscle Group:** _____

S M T W T F S **Start Time**_____
◯ ◯ ◯ ◯ ◯ ◯ ◯

Weight:_____ **Finish Time**_____

☐ **Upper Body** ☐ **Lower Body** ☐ **Abs**

Exercise	Set	1	2	3	4	5	6	7
	Reps							
	Weight							
	Reps							
	Weight							
	Reps							
	Weight							
	Reps							
	Weight							
	Reps							
	Weight							
	Reps							
	Weight							
	Reps							
	Weight							
	Reps							
	Weight							

Cardio	Time	Distance	Heart Rate	Cals Burned

Measurements

Neck	R Bicep	L Bicep	Chest	Waist	Hips	R Thigh	L Thigh	Calf

Date: _____ **Muscle Group:** _____

S M T W T F S   **Start Time** _____
◯ ◯ ◯ ◯ ◯ ◯ ◯

Weight: _____ **Finish Time** _____

☐ **Upper Body**   ☐ **Lower Body**   ☐ **Abs**

Exercise	Set	1	2	3	4	5	6	7
	Reps							
	Weight							
	Reps							
	Weight							
	Reps							
	Weight							
	Reps							
	Weight							
	Reps							
	Weight							
	Reps							
	Weight							
	Reps							
	Weight							
	Reps							
	Weight							

Cardio	Time	Distance	Heart Rate	Cals Burned

Measurements

Neck	R Bicep	L Bicep	Chest	Waist	Hips	R Thigh	L Thigh	Calf

Date:_____ Muscle Group: _____

S M T W T F S
○ ○ ○ ○ ○ ○ ○   Start Time_____

Weight:_____ Finish Time_____

☐ Upper Body   ☐ Lower Body   ☐ Abs

Exercise	Set	1	2	3	4	5	6	7
	Reps							
	Weight							
	Reps							
	Weight							
	Reps							
	Weight							
	Reps							
	Weight							
	Reps							
	Weight							
	Reps							
	Weight							
	Reps							
	Weight							
	Reps							
	Weight							

Cardio	Time	Distance	Heart Rate	Cals Burned

Measurements

Neck	R Bicep	L Bicep	Chest	Waist	Hips	R Thigh	L Thigh	Calf

Date:_____   **Muscle Group:**_____

S M T W T F S   **Start Time**_____
○ ○ ○ ○ ○ ○ ○

Weight:_____   **Finish Time**_____

☐ **Upper Body**   ☐ **Lower Body**   ☐ **Abs**

Exercise	Set	1	2	3	4	5	6	7
	Reps							
	Weight							
	Reps							
	Weight							
	Reps							
	Weight							
	Reps							
	Weight							
	Reps							
	Weight							
	Reps							
	Weight							
	Reps							
	Weight							
	Reps							
	Weight							

Cardio	Time	Distance	Heart Rate	Cals Burned

Measurements

Neck	R Bicep	L Bicep	Chest	Waist	Hips	R Thigh	L Thigh	Calf

Date: _____ **Muscle Group:** _____

S M T W T F S **Start Time** _____
◯ ◯ ◯ ◯ ◯ ◯ ◯

Weight: _____ **Finish Time** _____

☐ **Upper Body**   ☐ **Lower Body**   ☐ **Abs**

Exercise	Set	1	2	3	4	5	6	7
	Reps							
	Weight							
	Reps							
	Weight							
	Reps							
	Weight							
	Reps							
	Weight							
	Reps							
	Weight							
	Reps							
	Weight							
	Reps							
	Weight							
	Reps							
	Weight							

Cardio	Time	Distance	Heart Rate	Cals Burned

Measurements

Neck	R Bicep	L Bicep	Chest	Waist	Hips	R Thigh	L Thigh	Calf

Date: _____ **Muscle Group:** _____

S M T W T F S
○ ○ ○ ○ ○ ○ ○

Start Time _____

Weight: _____

Finish Time _____

☐ Upper Body ☐ Lower Body ☐ Abs

Exercise	Set	1	2	3	4	5	6	7
	Reps							
	Weight							
	Reps							
	Weight							
	Reps							
	Weight							
	Reps							
	Weight							
	Reps							
	Weight							
	Reps							
	Weight							
	Reps							
	Weight							
	Reps							
	Weight							

Cardio	Time	Distance	Heart Rate	Cals Burned

Measurements

Neck	R Bicep	L Bicep	Chest	Waist	Hips	R Thigh	L Thigh	Calf

Date:_____ **Muscle Group:** _____

S M T W T F S **Start Time**_____
○ ○ ○ ○ ○ ○ ○

Weight:_____ **Finish Time**_____

☐ **Upper Body**   ☐ **Lower Body**   ☐ **Abs**

Exercise	Set	1	2	3	4	5	6	7
	Reps							
	Weight							
	Reps							
	Weight							
	Reps							
	Weight							
	Reps							
	Weight							
	Reps							
	Weight							
	Reps							
	Weight							
	Reps							
	Weight							
	Reps							
	Weight							

Cardio	Time	Distance	Heart Rate	Cals Burned

Measurements

Neck	R Bicep	L Bicep	Chest	Waist	Hips	R Thigh	L Thigh	Calf

Date:_____ Muscle Group: _____

S	M	T	W	T	F	S
◯	◯	◯	◯	◯	◯	◯

Start Time_____

Weight:_____ Finish Time_____

☐ Upper Body ☐ Lower Body ☐ Abs

Exercise	Set	1	2	3	4	5	6	7
	Reps							
	Weight							
	Reps							
	Weight							
	Reps							
	Weight							
	Reps							
	Weight							
	Reps							
	Weight							
	Reps							
	Weight							
	Reps							
	Weight							
	Reps							
	Weight							

Cardio	Time	Distance	Heart Rate	Cals Burned

Measurements

Neck	R Bicep	L Bicep	Chest	Waist	Hips	R Thigh	L Thigh	Calf

Thank you!

WE ARE GLAD THAT YOU PURCHASED OUR BOOK!
PLEASE LET US KNOW HOW WE CAN IMPROVE IT!
YOUR FEEDBACK IS ESSENTIAL TO US.

Contact us at:

 log'Sin@gmail.com

JUST TITLE THE EMAIL 'CREATIVE' AND WE WILL

GIVE YOU SOME EXTRA SURPRISES!